God's COLORFUL Christmas

Jesus Was Born to Save

written by Esau McCaulley
illustrated by Rogério Coelho

TYNDALE KIDS

Tyndale House Publishers
Carol Stream, Illinois

Visit Tyndale's website for kids at tyndale.com/kids.

Visit the author's website at esaumccaulley.com.

God's Colorful Christmas: Jesus Was Born to Save

Designed by Jacqueline L. Nuñez

For manufacturing information regarding this product, please call 1-855-277-9400.

For information about special discounts for bulk purchases, please contact Tyndale House Publishers at csresponse@tyndale.com, or call 1-855-277-9400.

Library of Congress Cataloging-in-Publication Data

A catalog record for this book is available from the Library of Congress.

ISBN 979-8-4005-0103-6

Printed in China

32 31 30 29 28 27 26

7 6 5 4 3 2 1

The story of God and his plan to build his colorful Kingdom with people from all over the world is **THE BIGGEST AND GRANDEST STORY EVER TOLD**. In truth, it is the only story, and we are all living in it.

A long time ago, as part of his big story, God called someone to do a very important job. This person was a young woman named Mary.

Mary lived in a small town in Israel called Nazareth. She was an ordinary girl with ordinary dreams. SOMETIMES GOD CALLS ORDINARY PEOPLE TO DO BIG THINGS.

One day, God sent the angel Gabriel to visit Mary. (The name Gabriel means "God is a warrior." What a cool name for an angel.)

"Rejoice, you who are highly favored by God!" Gabriel said. "The Lord is with you!"

Mary wondered what Gabriel's words meant. What would make her favored by God? She was a poor girl in a small town in the middle of nowhere.

Gabriel told her, "Do not be afraid!" (That was easy for Gabriel to say–he was the angel, not the one meeting the angel!)

"Mary, you will give birth to a son," he explained. "You will name him Jesus. He will be called the Son of the Most High. HE WILL REIGN FOREVER, AND HIS KINGDOM WILL NEVER END."

This is the Kingdom and family God has been working toward since the beginning! It is a Kingdom that invites everyone to join. Whether you're rich or poor, young or old–no matter where you were born or the color of your skin–GOD'S COLORFUL KINGDOM WELCOMES YOU.

But Mary had an important question: "How can this happen if I'm not yet married?"

Gabriel answered, "Your child will be a miracle created within your body by the Spirit of God."

JESUS WOULD BE FULLY HUMAN AND FULLY GOD.
He is a walking mystery:
God in human flesh.

Mary knew it was important that God chose her. God didn't choose someone rich or powerful to raise his Son.

God does the opposite of what we expect all the time. He lifts up the poor, and he takes down those who believe they are stronger or wiser than God. Mary worshiped God because he keeps his promises and loves justice. We worship him for those exact same reasons today.

When it was almost time for Mary to give birth to Jesus, Caesar Augustus, the ruler of Rome, decided to count all the people he ruled. This included Mary and her husband, Joseph. Joseph was from the family of David, so he and Mary had to travel to Bethlehem—David's hometown—to be counted.

Jesus was not born in a fancy palace.

He was not surrounded by kings and servants.

His first meal did not come from a silver spoon.

Jesus was born surrounded by animals and ordinary people. He slept in a feeding trough. The most powerful being in the whole world–the Son of God–was a helpless baby who relied on his mother to meet all his needs.

GOD CAME CLOSE TO US SO THAT WE COULD COME CLOSE TO HIM, no matter how ordinary we feel.

And whom did God invite to celebrate the birth of his Son? Even more ordinary people.

On the night that Jesus was born, some shepherds were up late taking care of their flocks. Shepherds didn't get invited to parties for the rich and the famous. They weren't the first ones chosen for sports teams.

But God chose them to participate in the most important celebration ever: the day Jesus was born.

An angel of the Lord appeared to the shepherds. The glory of the Lord shone all around them. They were terrified.

Again, angels: wonderful, but scary.

The angel told them, "Do not be afraid. I bring good news. TODAY, IN DAVID'S CITY, A SAVIOR HAS BEEN BORN—the Messiah, the Lord! This will be the sign: you will find the baby wrapped in cloths and lying in a feeding trough."

The shepherds were amazed. What kind of King and Savior would be sleeping in a place used to feed animals?

The kind of King who knows and cares about people who struggle to find food and justice. The kind of King with a heart open to the world.

A few years later, Jesus and his family received more visitors. These visitors were not shepherds. They were wise men from far away, and they had been led to Bethlehem by a star. THEY CAME TO WORSHIP THE KING OF THE JEWS. When they found him, they gave him gifts of gold, perfume, and spices.

Lots of people saw Jesus in those days. Why does the Bible tell the story of people coming from a distant country to see him?

This part of the story reminds us what the big story is all about. God's plan was for the whole world.

The wise men were the first people from outside of Israel to seek Jesus, but they were not the last. God still brings people from all over the world to meet and worship his Son.

When Jesus arrived, he was surrounded by his family, animals, and shepherds. He was visited by strangers from far away.

BUT NO ONE HAS TO BE A STRANGER TO GOD.

He is a God for the people who feel stepped on and ignored. God is with us.

GOD WANTS EVERYONE TO BE PART OF HIS COLORFUL KINGDOM.

About the Author

Rev. Esau McCaulley, PhD, is associate professor of New Testament and the Jonathan Blanchard Chair of New Testament and Public Theology at Wheaton College in Wheaton, Illinois. Dr. McCaulley's research and writing focus is on New Testament exegesis, African American biblical interpretation, and public theology. He is the author of *How Far to the Promised Land: One Black Family's Story of Hope and Survival in the American South*, *Reading While Black: African American Biblical Interpretation as an Exercise in Hope*, *Josey Johnson's Hair and the Holy Spirit*, and *Andy Johnson and the March for Justice*. Dr. McCaulley is also a contributing opinion writer for *The New York Times*. His writings have appeared in *The Atlantic*, *The Washington Post*, and *Christianity Today*. He is married to Mandy, a pediatrician and Navy reservist. Together, they have four wonderful children.

About the Illustrator

Rogério Coelho lives in Curitiba, a city in the south of Brazil. He has worked as a professional illustrator for twenty-five years, illustrating more than one hundred books for Brazilian publishers, and has twice received the Jabuti Award (2012 and 2016), Brazil's most important literary award. In 2015, Rogério began illustrating for publishers in England (*Storytime Magazine*, a magazine aimed at children) and in the United States. His wordless picture book *Boat of Dreams* received starred reviews from *School Library Journal* and *Booklist*, was named a Best Book for Kids by the New York Public Library in 2017, and received the Independent Publisher Book Awards' gold medal for children's picture books. Rogério also illustrated *You Be You* (written by Richard Brehm), which received the same gold medal for children's picture books in 2021.